STARTERS SCIENCE

D1826145

Hot and Cold

Macdonald Educational

This boy is ill.
He feels hotter than usual.
The nurse is taking his temperature.
2

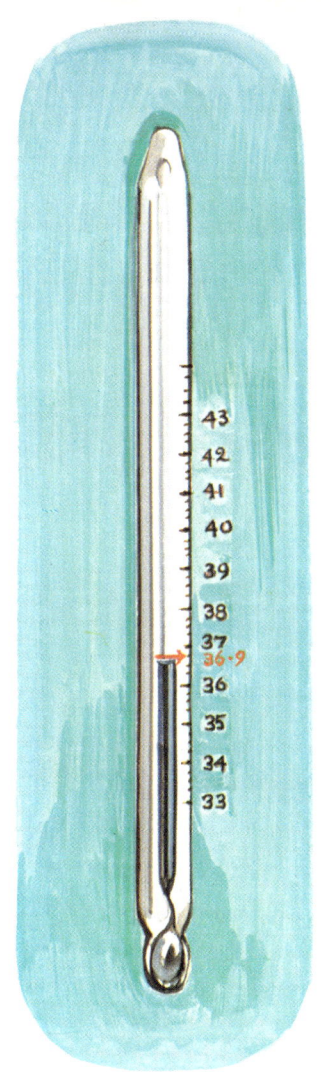

medical thermometer

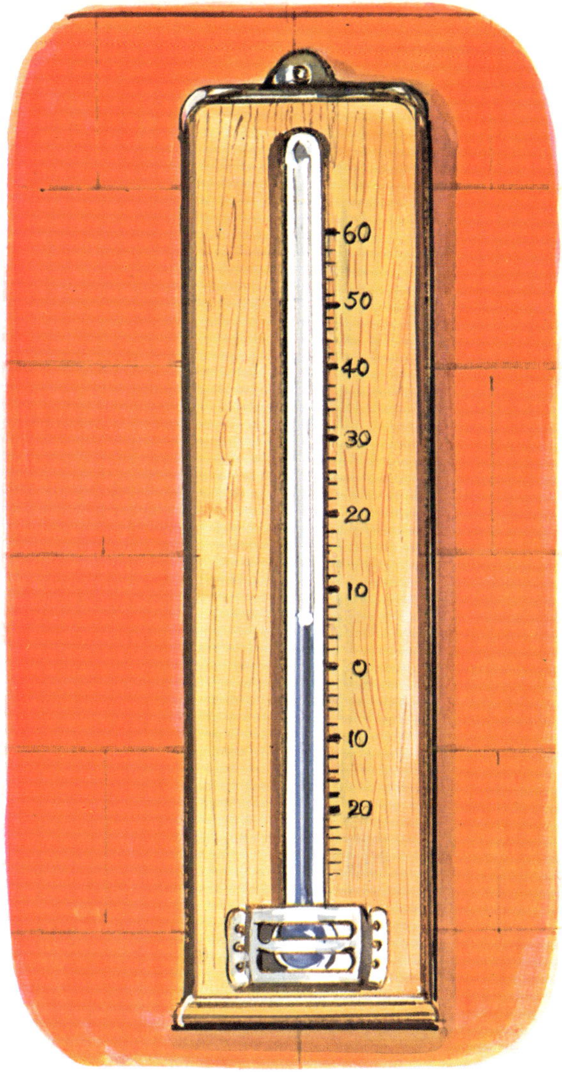

outdoor thermometer

There are two kinds of thermometers.
One goes in our mouth.
The other is used in rooms or outside.

3

The thermometer says twenty degrees.
The room feels nice and warm.

4

Test the temperature in different places.
Is it always the same?
Where is the coldest place?

In summer it is often hot.
In winter it is often cold.

strips of paper

You can make a chart like this.
Measure the temperature every morning.
Measure it outside, in the shade.
See how the temperature changes.

In some countries it is cold all the time.
In others it is hot all the time.

8

Deep inside the earth it is very hot.
Sometimes hot, melted rock
bursts out of the earth.
This makes a volcano.

It is a cold day.
The children wear winter clothes.
Their bodies are warm.
The clothes keep in the warmth.

10

1 hot water

2 woollen cloth

3 Later test the temperature of the water in both tins.

Fill two tins with hot water.
Wrap one in woollen cloth.
Test both temperatures later.
Try paper, cotton and plastic too.

11

hedgehog

dormouse

Some animals hide away all winter.
They become quite cold and stiff.
This is called hibernating.
They move only when the days get warmer.

12

Other animals move about
looking for food in winter.
This helps to make them warm.
Fur and feathers keep in the warmth.

13

Cooking pots and kettles
have special handles.
They do not let the heat go through
to your hand.

14

Put these things in hot water.
Now feel the top end of them.
Which ones let heat go through?
Which ones do not?

15

open fireplace

gas fire

electric fire

radiator

closed coke stove

There are many ways of heating buildings.
How is your home heated?
Find out how your school is heated.

water tank jacket

double glazed windows

glass fibre

We put thick jackets on hot water tanks.
We put glass fibre in the roof.
Some houses have double windows.
All these things help to keep heat in.

We need heat to cook food.

18

Food keeps best in a cold place,
like a fridge.

How cold is an ice-cube?
How long does it take to melt?

20

How can you keep an ice-cube
for longer?
Which way works best?

radiator

fan

Some engines have water to cool them.
Can you see the radiator and the fan?
They help to keep the water cool.

This is an electricity power station.
The huge towers cool the steam.
It changes back into water.

black paper

white paper

Try this for yourself on a sunny day.
Which thermometer rises higher?
How much difference is there?

On sunny days light coloured clothes
are cool to wear.
They keep out the heat.
Dark clothes take in more heat.

25

Rubbing makes things hotter.
Your hands get warm.
The cycle brakes get hot.
So do the saw and the nail.

heat shield

The space capsule travels very fast
as it falls back to earth.
It becomes very hot.
It has a heat shield at the front.

Index

 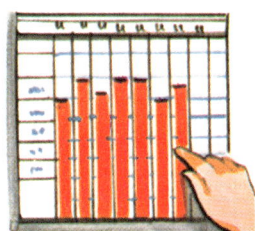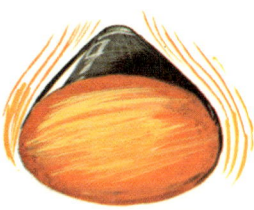